Humorous Poems
for
Children

By Daya Callan

Illustrated By Sushila Oliphant

AuthorHouse™
1663 Liberty Drive
Bloomington, IN 47403
www.authorhouse.com
Phone: 1-800-839-8640

Published by AuthorHouse 1/16/2012

ISBN: 978-1-4490-2111-5 (sc)

Library of Congress Control Number: 2009908713

Author's web address: www.thecallancollections.com
Cover Design: Artwork by Daya Callan, arrangement and layout by Sushila Oliphant
Book Layout, Design and Illustrations by Sushila Oliphant of Harmonic Designs:
www.harmonicdesigns.com & www.sushilaoliphant.com

This book is printed on acid-free paper.

authorHOUSE®

I dedicate this book to my wondrous angels,

who provided the inspiration to write these poems,

to every child and to every inner child

who dwells within us all.

ACKNOWLEDGEMENTS

This book was made possible because of the inspiration of my angels, the antics of my family members, the delightful encouragement of Ellen Fuir, my brother's incredible audience over the years, and the playfulness from The Light Brigade Poetry Group; years of listening to stories from Eastern scriptures, Folk Tales of India and Arabian Nights and from all of you who sat quietly while I read my poetry. I thank my wonderful friend, and artist, Sushila Oliphant. Because of her persistent questions and her amazing insight, I gained a better perspective on how to publish my collection of poems.

TABLE OF CONTENTS

TABLE OF CONTENTS

THE SNEAKS

*T*ick and Flea snuck stealthily
amidst the foresty fur.
They bit a snack
from Great Dane's back
until they heard a "GRRRR!"

THE CHEWING GUM

Bailey stepped in chewing gum.
It stuck upon his shoe.
And so, he tried to get it off
'cause it was yucky doo.

He scraped his shoe upon the wall
of a department store.
He scraped it on the sidewalk edge,
and then upon the door.

He rubbed his shoe along the glass,
and then upon the knob.
So, finally some of it came off
in one big, sticky glob.

By then, the gum had stretched like string
from sidewalk to the door,
along the wall and window pane,
and then across the floor.

People coming down the hall
and out the double door
got tangled in the gooey mess
and stretched it even more.

It clung to every lace and shoe;
it stuck to slacks and socks;
to dresses, ties and buckle belts;
to earrings and to locks.

It stuck to freshly polished nails;
to hair spray and to bows;
to lashes, buttons, collars, clips;
to stockings and to toes.

People stepped this way and that.
They twirled and whirled about.
They twisted, turned, and spun around,
attempting to get out.

They bumped their heads and poked their eyes,
determined to unglue
the sticky gum upon their clothes
all 'cause of you-know-who.

Bailey tried to help them out.
He pushed and pulled each one.
He yanked and pried each person there.
He even made them run.

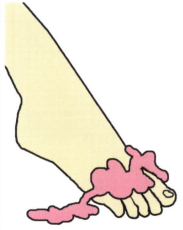

He had them step up very high,
then had them duck down low.
He made them crawl upon all fours;
he pushed them to and fro.

The gum just twanged them back again,
that group of twenty-three.
Four hours had then come and gone,
and still not one was free.

He had them bend this way and that
to rid them of that goo.
But tangled gum got everywhere;
whatever would he do?

Then Bailey stretched the gum way back
for one last, desperate shot
and sent them flinging here and there
across the parking lot.

THE PING-PONG BALL

*B*ailey threw a ping pong ball
to see what it would do.
It bonked upon his father's tooth,
and then it hit his shoe.

It bounced off all the hallway doors
and hit the cook's buffet.
That caused a splatter everywhere,
leaving disarray.

6

It pinged off all the crystal ware,
and then it hit his mom.
It boinked upon her cheek and knee,
then bopped his cat named Tom.

His mother took a broom to him.
He tried to tell her no.
She missed and hit the ball instead.
This *really* gave it go.

It hit the wall and tabletop
and broke the window pane.
His father caught it in his hand
and threw it down the drain.

It travelled through the sewer pipes
right out someone's commode;
swatting her upon the rear
leaving a mark that showed.

It doinked upon the sink and tub
and then it hit the light
and caused fluorescents to explode;
that really caused a fright.

The person that was sitting down
was now upon the floor,
and when it hit her on the head,
she clamored out the door.

It hit three walls and broke the screen
and flew across the yard.
The neighbors playing tennis there
bopped it very hard.

That sent it sailing miles away
to a garden guild.
It left behind some splattered plates
and bowls of punch that spilled.

A person startled, threw his plate;
cold cuts went here and there.
Then the ball went flying off
to who knows what or where.

DON'T WORRY

Measles and mumps and chicken pox, too;
bumpity heads and even the flu;
stuffity noses, fevers, head lice;
teeth growing in, scraped knees bandaged twice;
broken down toys, clunked elbows and wheezes;
bumped up behinds and slobbery sneezes;
drips and drools and food on the floor;
lollypop gooket and gum on the door...

Don't worry, don't worry, these things disappear
once they have reached their 25th year.

A GROUCH AND A GRUMP

*T*here once was a grouch and a grump
who went climbing around in the dump.
They found some old gook
they decided to cook,
and now they are both rather plump.

THE NOSE

*B*ailey's nose went on an adventure
and poked itself into a pie
that belonged to Enemy Neighbor.
Bailey now, has the biggest black eye.

WHAT HAPPENS

From window's ledge that views the street,
she threw on heads below
cake mix and rice and flour, too,
to see where it would go.

She's only three years old, you see,
and wonders 'bout such things:
Does it fly? How does it land?
What happens when one flings?

THE FRUIT PLATTER

*T*here are all types of fruit
on our dining room platter;
some oranges, grapes,
strawberries fatter,
lemons, some kiwis,
and cherries that matter,
apples, melons, even a pear.

But why is a burnt banana there?

HELLO?

*H*ello? Hello? Is anyone there?
I know you are inside somewhere.
I know that you don't really care
to have a moment's time to spare.

Hello? Hello? Is that you, Joan?
I only called you for a loan.
Could I have ever really known
you'd leave me with the answer phone?

Hello? Hello? Can anyone chat?
I simply called to tell you that
my aunt and uncle had a spat.
Do answer now; don't be a brat!

Hello? Hello? You there at all?
Who could ever have the gall?!
If you don't answer when I call,
I'll ring that telephone out of the wall!

Hello? Hello? Can anyone hear?
I'm calling now to make it clear
that when you finally answer, dear,
I'll clunk that phone right in your ear!

THE BALLET

We enter wooden, double doors
and step upon the marbled floors.
Cathedral ceilings high above
and statues of a white-winged dove.

Gentlemen so stately stand,
suited, tied and cuffed of hand.
Ladies move about with grace
ribboned, bowed and donned in lace.

Not on the floor or in a chair
a speck of dust is anywhere.
The wood and brass are buffed and bright,
glowing under muted light.

Every hair in perfect place
a smile so slight upon each face.
Our clothes are crisp, pressed and starched.
We're poised and still, our backs are arched.

The stage is set, the lights aglow.
All eyes are on the drapes just so.
Not a word is spoken here.
Silence enters every ear.

But then, from somewhere in the back,
we hear a click and then a clack.
We dare not even turn our heads,
this attitude we hold in dread,
because it would not be polite
to show that we suspect what might ...

The curtain rises to the call.
Lights are lowered in the hall.
And in that moment we're impressed
by stage performers finely dressed.

With splendid pomp begins a dance.
As we observe, they twirl and prance.
And to the melody so sweet
they spin upon their pointed feet.

But then, from somewhere in the back
comes a hiss and then a whack.
We dare not even turn our heads,
this attitude we hold in dread,
because it would not be polite
to show that we suspect a fight.

And on the stage the dancers fly-
pirouettes and leaps so high.
Enraptured by their spell we see
how they dance so gracefully.

But then from somewhere in the back
comes a scream and then a crack.
But now, *my* poise abandoned me.
I'm only six years old, you see.
I stood upon my chair, a brat,
and screeched at them, "Do not do that!"

FLOWER PETALS

*F*lower petals drift through the gaps
to cheer up all of the frowns,
leaving decorative little caps
on unsuspecting crowns.

SLY SPY

*T*he landlord decided to spy.
In the night, he'd just come on the sly.
On all fours he would creep;
behind bushes he'd peep.
Then he met his fate by and by.

In the bush was our cat, Arrowroot
who hissed at the sight of his boot.
He gave her a scowl,
so she spat on his jowl,
then he slapped her upon her small snoot.

She struck with a furious claw
left and right across his gnarled jaw,
as she reared to impress,
her point with finesse.
Then he swung his cap at her paw.

Was a grand and glorious fight.
And would have continued all night,
but they fell on the dog
and expanded this bog.
So now, there were three in the plight.

We heard a hiss and a growl;
a squeak, a spit and a howl;
a punch and a snap;
a bite and a slap;
a yelp, a "Help!" and a yowl.

They rolled through the bushes and mud,
then the three came down with a thud.
They clunked and they clanked,
they pulled and they yanked,
and then landed in some type of crud.

They bumped the hive of some bees.
Then we heard terrific "YEOWWWEEEES !"
Stung from toe to forehead,
they all scattered and fled,
so *that* just took care of all three!

THE TOE

*T*here once was a toe
who decided to show
her most extravagant poses.

She danced and she bowed
in front of a crowd,
but they ran away holding their noses.

A ROTTEN SACK OF POTATOES

There's a rotten sack of potatoes
in the refrigerator drawer.
My brother won't go get it;
he just slammed his bedroom door.
My sister pinched her nose and
said that there's no way.

So, then I asked my father;
he said, "No, not today."

And when I asked my mother,
she said to me, "My sweet,
if someone doesn't get it,
I guess we just won't eat."

33

MY ROOM

My mom has just discovered
chaos within my room
and handed me a mop and rag,
a bucket, and a broom.

The dresser drawers are open
and clothes are draped just so.
It's just that I'm in such a rush
and I'm always on the go.

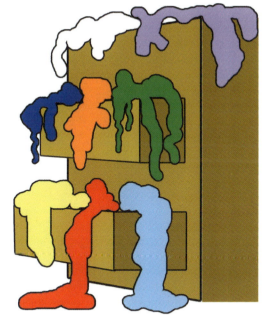

The dust has now collected
in clumps under my bed,
but that's for my experiment:
"Things Now Alive, Once Dead."

I have a hanging lantern
of cobwebs right up there.
And when adults come in my room,
they always stand and stare.

My closet doors are yawning
and everything's on the floor.
It's all within such easy reach.
I don't have to close the door.

And in my drawers I'm saving
some lunch from yesterday.
I've kept it in my school desk;
the kitchen's far away.

I've spiders in the corners,
and roaches run around.
I feed them crumbs from sandwiches
you'd better not sit down.

But, I have just remembered
what Mom has said to me:
I'm in here 'til I clean it up
if it means I'm ninety-three.

TRASH

THE APARTMENT MAILBOX

*T*he mail-order firms have gone bonkers.
They've sent me their large catalog.
Because of my high credit rating,
they think I'm a merchandise hog.

So, when I go open my mailbox,
I put my right foot on the wall
to yank out the junk mail and letters.
But, what if one day I should fall?

I may find myself flying backward
and land on the laundry room floor
or collapse in someone's clothes basket
or clunk against someone's front door.

Or maybe I'll fall in the dryer!
That's not how I'd like my clothes done.
And if it was open and empty,
you think I'd get out of that one?

Now, what if one day when I'm falling,
the neighbor should open his door
and I knock him right through his entrance?
It isn't polite. That's for sure!

So, please don't fill up my mailbox
with all of that mail-order junk.
'Cause who knows when I will fall backward.
There's no way to know who I'll clunk!

THE MAGICAL GARDEN

The fairies are floating high over
the horses who stand there below.
Some leaves surrounding the scenery
are higher than flowers that grow.
Some flowers are growing much higher
than fairies who fly in the air.
And horses are higher than flowers
as well as some leaves that they share.
So, here is the puzzling question:
Is a hierarchy there?

WHAT IF

What if you could walk
into anyone's house
and take whatever you find?
Go through their drawers
closets and rooms
and leave a great mess behind?

Then people would choose
the richest one's home,
and all would crowd through the door.
They'd push and they'd shove,
kick everyone's shins
to be sure they got more and more.

They'd pull others' hair
and step on their toes
and screech at the top of their voices.
The weaker ones then
would get out of the way
because they had no other choices.

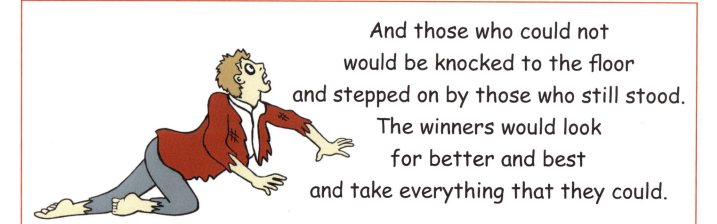

And those who could not
would be knocked to the floor
and stepped on by those who still stood.
The winners would look
for better and best
and take everything that they could.

Now here it is where
a pinch and a shove
would come to a bite and a scratch.
And a sneak and a steal
and a twist of the ear
would end in a double eye-patch!

By now most would be
bedraggled and bruised
and wounded upon the hard floor.
The few that were left
still standing at all
would be lugging things out the back door.

But then there would come
a time for them all
to now see what one would have guessed.
They all would reflect
on decisions they made
and conclude they were not at their best.

MOM WON'T CLEAN OUR FRIGIDAIRE

Mom won't clean our Frigidaire.
There's something, something growing there.
A rotten, sunken, apple core;
green, moldy cheese that's fuzzy or
old, sloshy salad, soggy bread,
and slimy, yucky things I dread.

Potato eyes poke out the door,
so now our house stinks even more
than Garbage Alley City Dump,
because there's some, big, moldered clump
of something, something growing there,
'cause Mom won't clean our Frigidaire.

Now, in the night I hear a "Clink!"
of who knows what; I dare not blink!
More time goes by and I can't bear
that Mom won't clean our Frigidaire.

CLUNK!! PLINK!

PING! PLUNK!!

Just last night I heard a "Clunk!"
A "Ping," a "Plink," and then a "Plunk!"
What should I do? Should *I* go see?
What climbs around inside? Yeoweee!

Months and months and months have passed,
and visitors are left aghast.
The doors and sides have bulged out wide
from something growing there inside!

Something, something's there alright;
I hear it growling in the night!
The box rocks back and forth and then,
it creeks and cracks and rocks again!

Police were called to stage a raid,
but they were all too much afraid!
And so we're left in great despair
'cause Mom won't clean our Frigidaire!

More months and months and months have passed!
I heard a roar just evening last!
What should I do? Should *I* go see?
What dreadful thing's in there? Yeoweee!

And so, and so, I finally dare
to see what *is* inside of there.
I creep up to the door one night
and fling it wide to such a sight!
And when I do, I can't stop yelling!
What do I see? I'm not telling.

THE COCKROACH

Mrs. Eden isn't there.
She found a cockroach in her hair.
When people turned around to stare,
they found her running everywhere.

Some people tried to calm her down,
but *how* she slapped and flung around,
then tugged and pulled and tore her gown,
and you could hear her 'cross the town.

Someone then reached to take it out,
but all she did was scream and shout,
and yelled and yelled, "Get out! Get out!"
flinging arms and legs about.

That roach with furry feet held tight
while she shook with all her might
and scattered people left and right
in desperate hopes to end her plight.

Swinging from the chandelier,
she heard a crackle in her ear,
and bringing on more waves of fear,
she kicked so much, no one came near.

But that roach would not let go!
It clung with every fuzzy toe.
She threw her purse and cried, "No! No!"
causing us to duck down low.

Because she had to have more space,
we left her the entire place.
We just could not keep up the pace
of that long and ragged race.

Now, just in case you want to know,
that happened in the church on Roe.
And now she will not even go
unless she brings her garden hoe.

The End!